Witness to History

The Troubles in Northern Ireland

Tony Allan

Heinemann
LIBRARY

www.heinemann.co.uk/library
Visit our website to find out more information about **Heinemann Library** books.

To order:

 Phone 44 (0) 1865 888066

Send a fax to 44 (0) 1865 314091

Visit the Heinemann Bookshop at www.heinemann.co.uk/library to browse our catalogue and order online.

First published in Great Britain by Heinemann Library,
Halley Court, Jordan Hill, Oxford
OX2 8EJ, part of Harcourt Education.

Heinemann is a registered trademark of
Harcourt Education Ltd.

© Harcourt Education Ltd 2004
First published in paperback in 2005
The moral right of the proprietor has been asserted.

Produced for Heinemann by Discovery Books Ltd
Editorial: Patience Coster, Nancy Dickmann and Tanvi Rai
Design: Ian Winton
Map artwork: Stefan Chabluk
Picture research: Rachel Tisdale
Production: Séverine Ribierre

Originated by Dot Gradations Ltd, UK
Printed and bound in China
by South China Printing Company

The paper used to print this book comes from sustainable resources.

ISBN 0 431 17067 3 (hardback)
08 07 06 05 04
10 9 8 7 6 5 4 3 2 1

ISBN 0 431 17072 X (paperback)
09 08 07 06 05
10 9 8 7 6 5 4 3 2 1

British Library Cataloguing in Publication Data
Allan, Tony 1946–
The troubles in Northern Ireland. – (Witness to History)
941.6 ' 0824

A full catalogue record for this book is available from the British Library.

Acknowledgements
The publishers would like to thank the following for permission to reproduce photographs:
Bettmann/Corbis: pp. **8**, **20**, **40**; Corbis Sygma: p. **7**; Hulton-Deutsch Collection/Corbis: pp. **19**, **23**, **24**, **36**, **38**, **50**; Leif Skoogers/Corbis: p. **34**; Mary Evans Picture Library: p. **10**; Paul Seheult: p. **7**; Eye Ubiquitous/Corbis: p. **6**; Polak Matthew/ Corbis Sygma: p. **46**; Popperfoto: pp. **4**, **26**, **28**, **30**, **33**, **35**, **42**, **43**, **44**, **45**, **48**; Richard Cummins/Corbis: p. **51**; Topham Picturepoint: pp. **9**, **12**, **14**, **16**, **17**, **18**.

Cover photograph shows the British army with riot shields and batons in a street in Northern Ireland, reproduced with permission of Alain Le Garsmeur/Corbis.

The publishers would like to thank Bob Rees, historian and Assistant Head Teacher, for his assistance in the preparation of this book.

Every effort has been made to contact copyright holders of any material reproduced in this book. Any omissions will be rectified in subsequent printings if notice is given to the publishers.

Words appearing in the text in bold, **like this**, are explained in the glossary.

Contents

The Troubles

Soldiers in battle gear running down residential streets; bodies covered with blankets following a bomb blast; angry crowds at victims' funerals. From 1969 onwards, for almost thirty years, such images dominated news coverage of Northern Ireland. The murderous civil disturbances known as 'the Troubles' blighted the lives of a generation of Northern Ireland's inhabitants, and the fears and divisions that caused them are still evident today.

The Troubles are rooted in the split between the Protestant and Catholic communities, which can be traced back at least four hundred years. At that time, Ireland was under the rule of Britain – a kingdom made up of England, Wales and Scotland. Ireland was not willing to be governed from abroad. In the 16th century, when Britain adopted the Protestant faith, the Irish people remained Catholic. Following an unsuccessful rebellion against British rule, Scottish Protestant settlers were deliberately moved to Ireland on the orders of the British king. They were 'planted', or settled, in **Ulster**, the region where the rebellion had been centred. The presence of the settlers was intended to counteract the influence of the resident Catholic population, which was considered disloyal to the British **Crown**.

In 1921 Ireland won independence from Britain. However, six of the nine counties that made up Ulster opted not to join the new Irish nation but to remain part of the **United Kingdom (UK)**. By no coincidence, all had a Protestant majority in their populations. In the years that followed,

Wielding batons and wearing riot gear and protective helmets, British troops move into action in the Bogside district of Londonderry in 1970. The British army was first called into the conflict in the previous year.

the rest of Ireland chose to live in a mainly Catholic **republic**, with an appointed president as its head of state. But the people of the six counties (known from 1920 as Northern Ireland) remained mostly Protestant and loyal to the Crown.

Second-class citizens

However, there were also large Catholic minorities in Northern Ireland. In principle they were granted full **civil rights**. In practice, however, they soon came to feel that they were treated as second-class citizens. The government of Northern Ireland was structured in such a way that all decision-making rested in Protestant hands.

A map of the United Kingdom, showing Northern Ireland as a province separate from the rest of Ireland (Irish Republic).

Yet the Protestants had worries of their own. Although they made up the majority of the Northern Irish population, they remained a minority in Ireland as a whole. They knew that **militant nationalists** throughout Ireland were demanding its **reunification** under a **republican** government. They wished to prevent that outcome at all costs.

So the background to the Troubles took shape. On one side was Northern Ireland's Protestant majority. The Protestants described themselves as **unionist**, because they supported union with the UK, and **loyalist**, because they remained loyal to the British Crown. On the other side was the Catholic minority, who described themselves as republican or nationalist. Although the two sides bore the labels of 'Protestant' and 'Catholic', religion had less to do with their differences than the social, political and economic divide that existed between two hostile communities.

5

How do we know?

People learn about the past in different ways. Most read about it in books written by historians who usually were not present at the events they describe. Historians tend to rely instead on earlier books for their information, or perhaps on documents from the time (see pages 9 and 17). However accurate their accounts may seem, they generally write about history at second hand. Therefore their works are known as 'secondary sources'.

Occasionally books may be written by people who were on the scene at the time (see pages 15, 23 and 27). These direct, eyewitness reports are called 'primary sources'. Today, some of the most vivid reporting appears in television or radio news broadcasts or in newspapers. Official documents, public records, diaries, letters, and evidence from law courts also provide first-hand raw material for future historians.

However, primary and secondary sources can both sometimes be misleading. People on the spot may not fully understand the events they are describing – or they may have a point of view that causes them to distort the way they report them. Historians and commentators may also be guilty of this distortion, known as 'bias'. Problems of bias are particularly acute in situations, like that of Northern Ireland, which split opinions sharply. Northern Ireland is a divided community, and people on either side of the divide often see the same events in a very different light.

In a Catholic area of Belfast, a wall painting proclaims solidarity between the **Irish Republican Army (IRA)** and the Palestine Liberation Organization. Left-wing **republicans** have always sought to link their own cause with those of other revolutionary movements worldwide.

There has never been a shortage of information about Northern Ireland's Troubles. Even so, a word often used to describe them is 'murky'. The truth has been obscured by the different biases shown by Protestants and Catholics alike, who have sought to present the facts in a way that supports their case.

On 30 December 1997, the funeral of Seamus Dillon takes place. He was a Catholic doorman gunned down outside the hotel where he worked. Seamus Dillon was shot by **loyalist** paramilitaries in a revenge killing for the murder of their leader, Billy Wright.

Silence and secrecy

The secrecy imposed by undercover warfare has further confused the issue. Politicians at least air their views openly, even if they sometimes slant their speeches to hide rather than reveal their real intentions. But **paramilitaries** – unofficial armed forces operating outside the law – must fight undercover, as must the security forces (army and police) whose job it is to track them. The paramilitaries need accurate information to identify targets. Equally, the security forces require it to track them down. Both sides therefore often spread 'disinformation' – intentionally inaccurate stories – to confuse and trap their opponents. In this atmosphere of deceit, some important questions about the events in Northern Ireland still go unanswered.

Nevertheless, the broad outlines of the conflict are well-documented. This book uses a combination of primary and secondary sources to record them. The text on the left-hand pages draws on published accounts to tell the story of the Troubles. On the right-hand pages, eyewitness accounts and important documents from both sides give a direct, first-hand view of particular historical moments. The aim is to allow you, the reader, to understand why things happened as they did and to make up your own mind about them.

An island apart

The tension between **loyalist** Protestants and **republican** Catholics in Northern Ireland is rooted in the distant past. Early in its history, Ireland had known a time of greatness. When most of Europe was caught in the grip of the **Dark Ages**, Irish monks and scholars had helped keep the light of learning aflame. Ireland was a centre of learning and art.

This manuscript illumination of St Matthew comes from the Book of Kells. Produced at Kells in central Ireland in the 8th century, this hand-illustrated Latin version of the Gospels is often regarded as the finest surviving example of early Celtic art.

Medieval Ireland was also renowned for its fighting men. The island was divided into separate kingdoms, which were involved in a seemingly endless round of wars. These internal divisions were to prove the nation's undoing in the year 1167, when an exiled king asked for English help in winning back his throne. King Henry II arrived at the head of an army in 1171, and from that time on the English never left.

From the start there were tensions between the English settlers and the resident Irish people. The communities remained quite distinct; at one time a law was even passed forbidding intermarriage between them. For the most part, English settlement was limited to a narrow strip of land centred on Dublin and known as the Pale. Residents there were expected to speak the English language and preserve English ways. The **Gaelic**-speaking Irish were kept, literally, beyond the Pale.

The English in Ireland

The following excerpt shows some of the laws introduced to medieval Ireland by the English. It is taken from a Statute of the Fortieth Year of King Edward III, and was brought into force by a parliament held in Kilkenny in 1367.

It is ordained and established that no alliance by marriage, fostering of children, concubinage [taking of lovers for payment] or amor [extramarital relationships] be henceforth made between the English and Irish ... and that no Englishman do give or sell to any Irishman, in time of peace or war, horses or armour, nor any manner of victuals [food] in time of war; and if any shall do to the contrary, and thereof be [found] guilty, he shall have judgement of life and member [the death sentence] as a traitor to our lord the king.

Also, it is ordained and established that every Englishman do use the English language, and be named by an English name, leaving off entirely the manner of naming used by the Irish; and that every Englishman use the English custom, fashion, mode of riding and apparel, according to his estate [class]; and if any English, or Irish living among the English, use the Irish language among themselves, contrary to the ordinance, his lands and tenements [landholdings], if he have any, shall be seized into the hands of his immediate lord, until he shall find sufficient surety to adopt and use the English language.

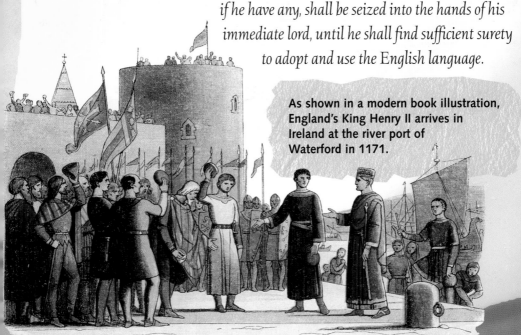

As shown in a modern book illustration, England's King Henry II arrives in Ireland at the river port of Waterford in 1171.

The plantation of Ulster

During the 16th century events occurred that left a permanent mark on the Irish political landscape. In the 1530s the **Reformation** split the Christian Church. England became a Protestant nation, while Ireland remained overwhelmingly Catholic. Shortly after, much of Europe was torn apart by wars between the new Protestant powers and the Catholic nations that remained loyal to the Pope.

Once England became a Protestant nation, the Catholic Irish feared religious persecution. These fears were realized when Queen Elizabeth I aggressively stepped up efforts to convert Ireland to Protestantism. As a result, the Irish Catholics became more united and anti-English than before. Their discontent boiled over in a series of revolts in **Ulster**, one of which allied the Earl of Tyrone, lord of Ulster, with Catholic Spain, England's greatest enemy at the time.

The rebellion was put down with much brutality, and the Earl's Ulster lands were seized by the **Crown**. To guarantee Ireland's future loyalty, Elizabeth's successor, King James I, 'planted' the country with Protestant settlers mostly from his own native land, Scotland. In doing so, he developed a policy already begun in Elizabeth's reign, when English nobles had been granted Irish lands. In Ulster, however, not just landowners but also tenant farmers came over, permanently changing the population structure of the province.

Early in the 17th century, King James I of Britain (right) made sure that areas of Northern Ireland were 'planted' with Scottish Protestant settlers.

These combinations and revoltes [gangs of rebels] have effected many execrable [dreadful] murders and cruelties upon the English, as well in the county of Limerick as in the counties of Cork and Kerry and elsewhere; infants taken from the nurse's breast and their brains dashed against the walls; the heart plucked out of the body of a husband in the view of his wife, who was forced to yield the use of her apron to wipe off the blood from the murderers' fingers; an English gentleman at midday in a town cruelly murdered, and his head cleft in several pieces; various people sent into Youghull among the English, some with their throats cut but not killed, some with their tongues cut out of their heads, others with their noses cut off; at the sight of which the English might the more bitterly lament the misery of their countrymen, and fear the like to befall themselves [fear that the same would happen to them].

And these execrable parts [dreadful deeds] are performed by the Irish tenants and servants of the English; and those that only yesterday were fed and nourished by the English are now the thieves that violently before their faces take from them their corn, cattle, and other goods; and the party spoiled [the injured party] thinks himself happy if he escape without loss of life, or other shameful villainy to himself, his wife or children; whereby it seems that it is a plot laid down by the traitors that every Irish next inhabiting should kill and spoil [rob] his English neighbour.

The Penal Laws

The 17th century also witnessed further violence in Ireland. In the 1640s Britain was torn apart by a civil war between the forces of Parliament and the king, Charles I. The parliamentary side was dominated by **Puritans** – extreme Protestants who hated Ireland's Catholics. In 1641, when the Puritans gained control of Ireland, Irish Catholics rose up in fury, launching a massacre of **Ulster** Protestants. As many as 12,000 people may have died. The parliamentary forces retaliated some years later, once the civil war in England had been won. An army under Britain's new ruler, Oliver Cromwell, travelled to Ireland to regain control, and committed fresh massacres of its own.

The pattern repeated itself later in the century, when Ireland backed the Catholic King James II against his Protestant rival, William of Orange. William decisively defeated James II at the Battle of the Boyne in 1690. His victory is commemorated to this day by Ulster Protestants, who are still known as Orangemen from the **Orange Order** that they set up in the following century to honour William's memory.

Following William's victory, a series of measures known as the **Penal Laws** were passed. These laws severely disadvantaged Irish Catholics; they were not allowed to hold public office, vote, join the army or go to university. More seriously still, they could not buy property. The result was that by the late 18th century the Catholics who made up the bulk of Ireland's population owned less than 5 per cent of its land. The so-called '**Protestant ascendancy**' over Ireland seemed to be almost complete.

England's ruler Oliver Cromwell lays siege to the Irish city of Drogheda in 1649, in this historical print. More than 2000 of the city's inhabitants died in the fighting.

The rule of law

The Penal Laws were a series of measures passed by the British Parliament to punish the Irish for supporting the deposed King James II and his heirs, who continued (unsuccessfully) to lay claim to the British throne. The Penal Laws made the Catholics, who were the vast majority of Ireland's population, very much second-class citizens in their own country.

From An Act to Restrain Foreign Education (1695)

Whereas it has been found by experience that tolerating at Papists [Roman Catholics] keeping school or instructing youth in literature is one great reason of many of the natives continuing ignorant of the principles of the true religion . . . no person of the Popish religion shall publicly teach school or instruct youth. . . upon pain of twenty pounds, and prison for three months for every such offence.

From An Act to Prevent the Further Growth of Popery (1703)

Every Papist shall be disabled to purchase any lands, or any rents or profit of lands, or any lease of lands, other than for a term not exceeding 31 years. . . No Papist shall inherit or take any other interests in land owned by a Protestant, unless the Papist shall conform to the Protestant religion within six months of the time at which he would be entitled to such lands. . . All lands owned by a Papist, and not sold during his lifetime for valuable consideration . . . shall descend . . . to all of his sons, share and share alike, and not to the eldest son only, and lacking sons, to all his daughters.

From An Act for the Better Regulating Elections of Members of Parliament (1745)

Every freeholder before voting, if required by one of the candidates or other voter, shall take an oath, which includes the following language: 'I am not a Papist, or married to a Papist, nor do I educate, or suffer to be educated, any of my children under the age of fourteen in the Popish religion.'

Emancipation and famine

In 18th-century Europe religious divisions gradually faded. In Britain, too, Protestant attitudes to Ireland's Catholics began to soften. By the end of the century, most of the **Penal Laws** had been **repealed**. Among Catholics and liberally-minded Protestants, an active movement for **emancipation** (restored **civil rights**) was under way. However, in 1801, following another unsuccessful rebellion in Ireland, the **Act of Union** was passed, making Ireland constitutionally a part of the **United Kingdom**, along with England, Scotland and Wales.

Emancipation was achieved in 1829. For the first time in centuries, Ireland's Catholic population had almost the same legal rights as the Protestants. But the years of oppression had left their mark. Most of the land still remained in Protestant hands, and the vast majority of Catholics worked as landless labourers renting plots of land from Protestant landlords.

The social divide was cruelly exposed by the Great Hunger of 1846–50. Caused by potato blight, a disease of the crop on which most poor Irish people depended for survival, this famine killed almost a million people and forced another 1.5 million (out of a total of 8 million) to **emigrate**. The burden fell almost entirely on the Catholics. The **Ulster** Protestants, who had access to oats, a traditional Scottish crop the 'planted' settlers had brought with them two centuries earlier, were little affected. The famine itself, and the ineffectiveness of government policies to **alleviate** it, fuelled fresh bitterness in the Catholic population. Meanwhile, mass emigration created a sizeable Irish-American community that was one day to play a part in the Northern Ireland crisis.

This illustration shows Irish peasants in the famine year of 1847. Furniture was a luxury in the poorer parts of Ireland at the time, and most people slept on the earth floor of their huts.

A terrible hunger

Nicholas Cummins, a magistrate of the city of Cork, visited the small town of Skibbereen in southern Ireland at the height of the Great Famine of 1846. He described what he saw in a letter that was published in *The Times* newspaper.

The Times

Being aware that I should have to witness scenes of frightful hunger, I provided myself with as much bread as five men could carry, and on reaching the spot I was surprised to find the wretched hamlet apparently deserted. I entered some of the hovels [dwellings] to ascertain the cause, and the scenes which presented themselves were such as no tongue or pen can convey the slightest idea of. In the first, six famished and ghastly skeletons, to all appearances dead, were huddled in a corner on some filthy straw, their sole covering what seemed a ragged horsecloth, their wretched legs hanging about, naked above the knees. I approached with horror, and found by a low moaning they were alive – they were in fever, four children, a woman and what had once been a man. It is impossible to go through the detail. Suffice it to say that in a few minutes I was surrounded by at least two hundred such phantoms, such frightful spectres as no words can describe, either from famine or from fever. Their demoniac yells are still ringing in my ears, and their horrible images fixed upon my brain. . .

A mother, herself in fever, was seen the same day to drag out the corpse of her child, a girl about twelve, perfectly naked, and leave it half covered with stones. In another house, within five hundred yards of the cavalry station at Skibbereen, the dispensary doctor found seven wretches lying unable to move, under the same cloak. One had been dead many hours, but the others were unable to move either themselves or the corpses.

Home rule for Ireland

The Great Famine revived Irish bitterness towards Britain. Many Irish people no longer just wanted equal rights: they wanted to rule their own country. In the 1850s some **radical nationalists** set up an organization called the **Fenian Brotherhood**. This was an armed group prepared to use bombings and **assassinations** to drive the British from Ireland. (The Fenian Brotherhood is often seen as the ancestor of today's **Irish Republican Army**.) In contrast, moderate nationalists sought separation by democratic methods in the campaign for **home rule**. This was the right for Ireland to run its own affairs while remaining within the **UK**. The supporters of home rule demanded the **repeal** of the **Act of Union** of 1801 and the establishment of an Irish parliament in Dublin.

An 1886 cartoon shows British Liberal Prime Minister William Gladstone (left), a supporter of Irish home rule, preparing to race his Conservative rival Lord Salisbury, who wanted Ireland to remain a full part of the United Kingdom.

The home rule movement won the support of the Liberal Party, one of the two great parties (the other being the Conservatives) that dominated British politics at the time. Twice, in 1886 and 1893, **government bills** backing home rule were put forward in the British Parliament in London by the Liberal Prime Minister William Gladstone, only to be defeated each time. In 1913 a third bill introduced by Gladstone's successor, Prime Minister Herbert Asquith, won the support of the House of Commons. Nationalists had reason to believe that their goal of self-government had almost been achieved.

Nobody told – and no one was spared

The home rule debate played out against a background of bitter disputes between mainly Protestant landlords and largely Catholic tenants. Writing in 1880, Mrs Craik describes one such confrontation in her book *An Unknown Country*.

Some years ago, in Glen Veagh was enacted a tragedy. A certain Mr Adair, a wealthy Scotsman, bought large tracts of land here, and had many contests with his tenants, with whom he was far from popular: being an absentee landlord, leaving his affairs to be administered by his agents, who probably understood the peculiarities of Irish nature as little as their master. One – no, more than one of them – was murdered. Then Mr Adair declared that, if in three months the murderers were not given up, he would **evict** all the inhabitants of the Glen.

Any person acquainted with Ireland can guess the result. Everybody knew, but nobody told. Much exasperated, Mr Adair kept his word. The innocent suffered with the guilty. Every family, women and children, young and old, was turned out on the moor – for eviction here, in this desolate place, means entire homelessness.

'And what became of them?' I asked.

'Some died, ma'am, and some settled in other parts. A good many went to America. Anyhow, there's not one o' them left here. Not one.'

'And Mr Adair?'

'He's dead.'

The man set his teeth together, and hardened his face – a face I should not like to meet in a lonely road. It was the first glimpse I had had, since our coming to Ireland, of that terrible blood-feud now existing between landlord and tenant, in which neither will see the other's rights – and wrongs; nor distinguish between the just and the unjust, the good and the bad.

Painting of police surveying the after-effects of an 1867 Fenian bombing aimed at freeing Irish captives from a London prison. Four people were killed in the blast.

Ulster will fight...

As the 20th century got under way, the Protestants of **Ulster** watched the agitation for **home rule** with growing alarm. They were very aware that Irish self-government would leave them in the minority in a Catholic-dominated country. They had grown used to holding a relatively privileged position in Irish affairs, and feared that the proposed changes would leave them disadvantaged.

The Protestants found a spokesperson for their cause in Sir Edward Carson, a Dublin-born lawyer and a Conservative Member of Parliament (MP). Carson was fiercely opposed to home rule, and as an influential politician with powerful connections he was able to make his voice heard. With the slogan 'Ulster will fight, and Ulster will be right', he organized a troop of 100,000 volunteers ready to resist home rule by armed force if necessary. The threat of civil war seemed real.

Pressure from Carson and his **Ulster Volunteer Force (UVF)** forced Prime Minister Herbert Asquith to propose a compromise over home rule. Each of the nine counties of Ulster, where the Protestant population was concentrated, should vote on the question of whether or not to accept the new arrangement. But in 1914, before a final deal could be reached, World War I broke out. The government decided to delay dealing with the questions of home rule and of Ulster's special position until the fighting was over.

With the Union Jack flag fluttering behind him, Sir Edward Carson (centre, with walking stick) is depicted inspecting armed members of the Ulster Volunteer Force (UVF) in 1914. The UVF was dedicated to keeping Ulster within the United Kingdom.

Opposing home rule

On 'Ulster Day' in 1912, **unionist** leader Sir Edward Carson became the first person to sign the 'Solemn League and Covenant', promising to resist home rule. In all, more than 471,000 **loyalists** eventually signed the document, rejecting the idea of forming part of a united Ireland.

Ulster's Solemn League and Covenant, Saturday, 28 September 1912

On Ulster Day 1912, Ulster unionists put their names to a covenant committing themselves to opposing home rule for Ireland, seeking instead to remain part of the United Kingdom.

Being convinced in our consciences that home rule would be disastrous to the material well-being of Ulster as well as of the whole of Ireland, subversive of our civil and religious freedom, destructive of our citizenship and perilous to the unity of the Empire, we, whose names are underwritten, men of Ulster, loyal subjects of his Gracious Majesty King George V, humbly relying on the God whom our fathers in days of stress and trial confidently trusted, do hereby pledge ourselves in solemn Covenant throughout this our time of threatened calamity to stand by one another in defending for ourselves and our children our cherished position of equal citizenship in the United Kingdom and in using all means which may be found necessary to defeat the present conspiracy to set up a Home Rule Parliament in Ireland. And in the event of such a parliament being forced upon us we further solemnly and mutually pledge ourselves to refuse to recognize its authority. In sure confidence that God will defend the right we hereto subscribe our names. And further, we individually declare that we have not already signed this Covenant.

GOD SAVE THE KING

The Easter Rising

Most moderate **nationalists** were content to wait out the war, not least because the case for **home rule** had been agreed in principle. However, a small minority of extreme **republicans** committed to total independence for Ireland saw the delay as evidence of British untrustworthiness. They thought the best hope for independence lay not with British promises but rather in taking advantage of Britain's weakness, bogged down as it was in fighting a world war.

The result was the Easter Rising of April 1916. About 2000 republicans seized the centre of Dublin and held it against British troops for five days. After that time the British army regained control of the city. The army also seized a consignment of German weapons that had been shipped to the republicans.

For the British, the Easter Rising was a clear case of treason in time of war, and it had to be severely punished. Accordingly, sixteen of its leaders were shot. The executions turned out to be a bad mistake. Previously, the rising had won little public support, but the executions made **martyrs** of the rebels and won sympathy for their cause. In the general election that followed World War I's end in 1918, the **Sinn Fein** ('We Ourselves') Party, which had supported the rising and was now dedicated to complete independence for Ireland, won a large majority of Irish seats.

British forces defend a barricade during street fighting in the Easter Rising of 1916. The uprising, which sought to establish an independent republican Ireland, was put down within a week.

Striking for freedom

On 24 April 1916, the first day of the rebellion, the leaders of the Easter Rising issued the following proclamation from Dublin's General Post Office, which they had seized as their headquarters. In it they described themselves as the provisional government of the **republic** they hoped to set up, and justified their action in taking up arms against the British administration.

The Provisional Government of the Irish Republic to the People of Ireland

IRISHMEN AND IRISHWOMEN: In the name of God and of the dead generations from which she receives her old tradition of nationhood, Ireland, through us, summons her children to her flag and strikes for freedom.

We declare the right of the people of Ireland to the ownership of Ireland, and to the unfettered control of Irish destinies, to be sovereign. . . The long **usurpation** of that right by a foreign people and government had not extinguished the right, nor can it ever be extinguished except by the destruction of the Irish people. In every generation the Irish people have asserted their right to national freedom and sovereignty; six times during the past three hundred years they have asserted it in arms. Standing on that fundamental right and again asserting it in arms in the face of the world, we hereby proclaim the Irish Republic as a Sovereign Independent State, and we pledge our lives and the lives of our comrades-in-arms to the cause of its freedom, of its welfare, and of its exaltation among the nations.

We place the cause of the Irish Republic under the protection of the Most High God, whose blessing we invoke upon our arms, and we pray that no one who serves that cause will dishonour it. . . In this supreme hour the Irish nation must, by its valour and discipline and by the readiness of its children to sacrifice themselves for the common good, prove itself worthy of the destiny to which it is called.

Partition

The rising tide of Irish nationalism had an important effect on **Ulster**, where the Protestant majority remained bitterly opposed to the idea of joining a united Ireland. There, the 1918 elections produced a firm **unionist** majority committed to keeping the link with Britain as spelled out in the 1801 **Act of Union**.

When fighting broke out between armed Irish **nationalists** and the British army in 1919, Ulster supported the British government and troops. The six counties took on the name of Northern Ireland and remained a part of the **UK**. By the Government of Ireland Act, passed in 1920, Northern Ireland acquired a parliament of its own and an executive (group) led by a prime minister with responsibility over local affairs. It also continued to send MPs to the British Parliament in London, so keeping a voice in matters affecting the entire UK. In effect, the island of Ireland had been partitioned (divided) into two separate, mutually suspicious sections.

The Anglo-Irish Treaty of 1921 ended the fighting between nationalists and the British army and gave virtual independence to Ireland. But the treaty excluded the six counties of Ulster with majority Protestant populations. Henceforth most of Ireland became the **Irish Free State**, with only a few remaining ties to Britain. These last links were removed, first in 1937-38, when a further treaty established Ireland as an entirely independent nation, and then in 1948-49, when remaining ties with the British **Crown** were severed and the country became the **Republic** of Ireland.

This map shows Ireland after 1920. It was divided into the Irish Free State and Northern Ireland. The six counties shown remained part of the UK.

Bad times

A farmer in County Fermanagh in southern Ulster describes the fighting between Irish nationalists and British soldiers that led up to the Anglo-Irish Treaty of 1921.

They put the curfew on because times went that bad, you see. These men, what you call the IRA or Republicans, they were digging trenches and putting bushes across the road, ambushing and shooting the soldiers from both sides. When they got them to come to the place where they had the bush across, they attacked on both sides and killed a lot of soldiers. That's what caused them to bring on curfew. If you were found out after it, you were liable to be shot. There was nobody caught about our side. It kept fairly quiet, only just that you wouldn't want to be out. . .

Well, you see as it is, maybe there's some of it going on today. If the Catholics knowed of a prominent man being busy with these English soldiers or anything, they would maybe go and burn his house. There was retaliation then: they would come and burn a Catholic house. So it never stopped until it went as far as the towns. In 1921 or thereabouts, that wee village beside us in Rosslea was burned to the ground. The Protestant people spilt petrol on the Catholic houses and burned them out, nearly every one of them.

The Irish nationalist leader Michael Collins (seated, right) poses with fellow republicans in 1920. Collins helped negotiate the treaty that set up the Irish Free State.

The Stormont system

The parliament that Northern Ireland acquired under the Government of Ireland Act was based at Stormont, a suburb of Belfast. From the start it was dominated by the **Ulster Unionist Party**, representing the Protestant majority and committed to continuing union with the **UK**.

Secure with their built-in parliamentary majority, the **unionists** set about arranging the political life of the province to suit their own interests. In some areas where the Catholic presence was strong, local council boundaries were redrawn to take in potential Protestant voters. This process – known as 'gerrymandering' – ensured that Protestants retained control locally as well as nationally. The councils then repaid the people who elected them by favouring Protestants in the allocation of public-sector jobs, council housing, and in the funding of education. Catholic opposition was kept in check by a largely Protestant police service supported by an armed **auxiliary** force, the **B Specials**, who were equipped to put down any public show of dissent by violent means.

Outnumbered two to one within Northern Ireland, the Catholics were resentful, but for more than forty years saw little hope of change. The British government in **Westminster** was generally sympathetic to the unionists' **loyalist** views and seemed reluctant to intervene in the internal affairs of the province. **Ulster** came to be seen as a small, self-contained world, operating largely according to its own rules.

In 1955, children light a fire for recreation in a poor district of Londonderry. Housing conditions were appalling in the city at the time, particularly in the Catholic neighbourhoods.

Social divisions
In the early 1960s, with his wife Patricia, Dr Conn McCluskey founded the Campaign for Social Justice to protest about anti-Catholic discrimination. Here he describes the situation at that time in his home town of Dungannon.

Most of the good shops were owned by Protestants. There were two factories in which the lower ranks of employees were Catholic, but they had no managerial representations in the factories. There were two secondary schools: St Patrick's, the Catholic institution, and the Protestant Royal, a fine school. But the difference between the Royal and St Pat's was that the people there [at the Royal] knew that its pupils were going to get the jobs when they were educated.

Because of what had happened before, the worst farms were in the mountainy parts and they were the Catholic farms. The good lowland farms were mostly Protestant because they had owned them since the sixteenth or seventeenth century. The picture was one of Catholic workmen looking after the roads under a Protestant supervisor or foreman.

Among solicitors and doctors there was a fair allowance on each side, because people could choose their school and they could choose their doctors. This was one of the few areas where there was equal treatment. It was a middle-class thing . . . there wasn't the opportunity to discriminate and the community got on well together.

The civil rights movement

In the 1960s the situation in Northern Ireland began to change. First, a liberally-minded **unionist**, Terence O'Neill, became Northern Ireland's prime minister and began trying to improve conditions for the Catholic minority. His policies aroused hostility within his own party, and outside parliament the Protestant reaction against his reforms quickly started to take shape.

1968 was a year of social upheaval and protest around the world. Following the example of Dr Martin Luther King Jr's campaign for black **emancipation** in the USA, a group of young protestors, most of them Catholic, had set up their own **civil rights** movement. It was dedicated to promoting equal treatment for all Northern Ireland's citizens by non-violent means. Now they began to stage public rallies.

The actions of the protestors stirred up a hornets' nest. Their demonstrations quickly became a target for Protestant anger. Television pictures of Protestant policemen beating peaceful demonstrators shocked people in mainland Britain. Early in 1969, when a protest march was ambushed outside Londonderry by **loyalists** armed with stones and cudgels, riots broke out in Catholic areas of the city in sympathy with the marchers. The slide into open violence had begun.

The 22-year-old Bernadette Devlin (third from left), was **Westminster's** youngest-ever Member of Parliament. Here she stages a sit-in with fellow members of Northern Ireland's civil rights movement outside 10 Downing Street, the British Prime Minister's London residence, in 1970.

Trouble in the fields

The civil rights movement in Ulster quickly stirred up a violent reaction from some sections of the Protestant community. In January 1969, a civil rights march from Belfast to Londonderry was ambushed by loyalists at Burntollet Bridge, apparently with help from the local police force. Here one of the marchers describes what he witnessed.

I saw the police moving through the fields, and then I saw the first attacker wearing a white armband. Then I began to see other men wearing similar armbands standing in groups on high ground along the road. I remember then dismissing the idea that the attackers would simply be angry groups of locals annoyed at demonstrators passing through their village. My impression now was that the attack was well organized, and the armbands were for recognition purposes.

By now the field seemed crowded with men and youths, perhaps a hundred or a hundred-and-fifty. I saw some women and girls, too, among the people in the field. I saw the police marshalling a girl along in the field. She carried two milk bottles in her hand. Then I saw the first stone come whizzing through the air and remember shouting to the people near me to get in against the hedge. In a second the air was thick with missiles. I pulled my coat up around my head and crouched down, stumbling forward. There was utter confusion as girls screamed, and stones and bottles crashed around. I kept my head down but on once looking up I saw another large group of men with cudgels and sticks running on to the road ahead of us. There was tremendous confusion as people stumbled and grabbed each other for cover and protection.

No Surrender!

Growing public concern over Catholic grievances in 1968 and 1969 made the Protestants fearful. Protestant **loyalists** knew that most Catholics would prefer to unite with the Irish Republic than with the **UK**. They were also suspicious of the intentions of the Republic of Ireland, where many people remained in favour of a united Ireland. In particular, they feared the **Irish Republican Army (IRA)**, an undercover organization dedicated to reuniting Ireland by force. The IRA had played a crucial role in the 1920s during the struggle for Irish independence, but because of its support for violence had subsequently been banned in the Republic of Ireland and in **Ulster**. Although it had not been very active in recent years, it was still feared by loyalists.

The **Ulster Volunteer Force (UVF)**, a loyalist **paramilitary** group, had been relaunched as early as 1966, before the start of the **civil rights** agitation. Now, in response to the perceived threat of the IRA and Catholic grievances, the UVF gained the support of more extreme **unionists**. Meanwhile, **militant** Protestantism found an unbending spokesperson in Ian Paisley, founder of the fiercely anti-Catholic Free Presbyterian Church, whose supporters protested angrily against the prospect of making any concessions to **nationalism** or **republicanism**. The watchwords of the Paisleyites were: 'No Surrender!'

In 1969 the Protestant backlash quickly turned violent. Loyalist groups wanting to undermine Terence O'Neill's reforming policies caused disruption by launching bomb attacks on power stations and on a reservoir. In the face of rising discontent in his own **Ulster Unionist Party**, the prime minister resigned.

In July 1970 Ian Paisley addresses fellow unionists after a parade celebrating the Protestant victory at the Battle of the Boyne in 1690, almost three centuries earlier. The Union Jack flag waves beside him.

A Protestant view

Speaking in the early 1990s, Edna Hanson, a resident of a housing estate in a Protestant area of Belfast, looks back at the Troubles and explains to an interviewer what she believes in and why she continues to support Ian Paisley.

I'm telling you exactly how I feel, and I'm not ashamed to do so: I'm for the Royal Family and the **Union Jack**, I'm a true Orange Loyalist, I always have been and I'm not ashamed of it.

All my uncles were in the war, fighting for the British, and so was my father. My grandparents too, they were upright religious people who wanted to lead good Christian lives. I was brought up to believe that the **Twelfth of July** was the greatest day in our calendar, when we always paraded with bands and flags and drums and Union Jacks, to celebrate King Billy's defeat of King James at the Battle of the Boyne. He made sure for ever afterwards that we were not going to be under Catholic domination, so just tell me what is wrong with that? The proudest date in our history, and yet now when we want to celebrate it by having parades and showing how proud of it we are, people say we're being provocative. . .

I love Mr Paisley because he stands up for all us Protestant people and our rights. He says to the British Government what needs to be said, he's not frightened of them and he speaks for all ordinary working-class people like me. He says, and he's right, that Catholics are always trying to interfere in Ulster affairs, and it needs to be said. . .

Oh yes, if necessary we'll sacrifice our lives. And others'? Well, what do you think? Don't misjudge the heart of Ulster men and women: we can't be frightened and we won't give in.

29

Sending in the troops

Throughout 1969, Northern Ireland drifted towards chaos. By **loyalist** tradition, the summer was the time for marches, organized by groups like the **Orange Order** and the **Apprentice Boys of Derry**. These groups had been set up in the distant past to commemorate 17th-century Protestant victories. Catholics had long resented the marches, and in the new atmosphere of **militancy** stirred up by the **civil rights** protests they met them with bricks, bottles and petrol bombs. The result in Londonderry was three days of rioting between Catholics and the police. This conflict became known as the Battle of the Bogside, after the Bogside housing estate where the trouble centred.

The riots were soon repeated on an even more devastating scale in Belfast, where guns were used for the first time in the Troubles (as the disturbances in Northern Ireland came to be called). So, too, were firebombs; in all, an estimated 300 Protestant and 1500 Catholic families were forced to flee their homes.

The local police forces were overwhelmed by the scale of the disorder. In despair, the Stormont government appealed to London for help. On 15 August 1969, the **UK**'s Labour Prime Minister Harold Wilson agreed to send in British troops to keep the peace. The hope was that they would be speedily withdrawn, but in fact they ended up staying for well over thirty years.

In August 1969, rioters carrying bottles, stones and batons charge police lines in Londonderry during the Battle of the Bogside – two days of civil strife that followed a Protestant march past this impoverished Catholic residential neighbourhood.

Posted to Northern Ireland
A soldier in the Cheshire Regiment of the British army describes the experience of arriving for a tour of duty in Northern Ireland in 1974 as an eighteen-year-old recruit.

I did not really have any views on Ireland before I became a soldier. All I can remember are the civil rights marches on the TV, the burning of houses and the population movement. I joined the regiment on a Tuesday, spent a long weekend at home and on the following Monday at 1800 hrs we sailed to Belfast. As for getting the situation explained, nothing was explained until after we were whisked off to Ballykinler [army base] to be trained for the streets. We were told that we were there to maintain law and order and to assist the civil powers. The cops were losing their grip, so we were there to support public order so that the Prods [Protestants] didn't batter the Catholics, who were shooting squaddies [soldiers] and cops. I'd just come out of training and it didn't register that people, including soldiers, were being injured and killed. In a way I was looking forward to coming to Ireland. It was a chance to prove myself, to try out the skills that I had learnt in training.

My first impressions as I got off the *Sir Galahad* [troopship] at 0600 hrs were: 'What is this place?' It was damp and miserable. There was loads of noise, shouting troops with black badges and loaded rifles. We were told to get on a four-ton lorry which went off through Belfast. My first view of Belfast brought it home to me that I might not come home again. Derelict housing estates, frightened, vulnerable people who went quiet as we passed. There seemed to be eyes everywhere, and amidst the chaos was the smell of peat fires. 'God,' I thought, 'I'll be glad to see the back of this place.'

Paramilitaries and protests

When they first arrived in Northern Ireland, the British troops were welcomed as protectors by the Catholic community. Housewives gave soldiers cups of tea on the street. Fearing the local police force as pro-Protestant, Catholics had earlier looked to their traditional champions in the **IRA** for protection, but they had received no response. Graffiti began to appear on walls in **nationalist** areas claiming: 'IRA = I Ran Away'.

All that soon changed. The same soldiers who initially had been viewed as guardians quickly came to be seen by the Catholics as oppressors. This was partly because of attitudes in the army itself. Here sympathies lay more naturally with **loyalist** Protestants, who supported Britain and the **Crown**, than with nationalist Catholics, whose loyalties were with Ireland. Equally important for the changing attitudes, however, were the **terrorist** activities of **republican** extremists.

> ### The Ballad of Gerry Kelly, Newsagent
> A poem by James Simmons (edited here for length) describes one of the murders that became common on both sides of the religious divide from 1969 onwards.

Disgusted by the IRA's failure to respond in the 1969 disturbances, a group of mostly younger **militants** set up a breakaway movement calling itself the **Provisional IRA** ('Provos' for short). From the start the Provos saw the British army as their main enemy, viewing it as an occupying force to be fought by bomb and bullet. In February 1971, the first British soldier was shot dead by the Provos, and other murders and bombings soon followed. The army responded by imposing **curfews** on Catholic areas and conducting house-to-house searches. By a sad irony, being treated as an oppressor made the army behave in an oppressive way.

Here's a song for Gerry Kelly,
Listen carefully and see
What's the moral of the story.
It makes no sense to me.

Worked ten hours six days a week,
Sundays closed at three.
They say he made a decent living.
Rather him than me.

Social centre for the neighbours—
Not much cash in that—
Buying fags or blades or tissues,
Waiting on to chat.

Sixty-nine the nightmare started.
Loyalist anger rose:
Sweet shops, butcher shops and pubs
Were burned down, forced to close.

One dark evening last November—
Turn the lights on till we see—
Gerry Kelly still in business,
Wife gone back to make the tea.

Sorting out the evening papers
While his son is selling sweets,
In our time, our town, two gunmen
Walk in off the streets.

* * * * * * * *

Civilians lined up against a wall are searched for hidden weapons by British troops in 1971. The army's presence was initially welcomed by Catholics, but heavy-handed tactics and IRA propaganda soon combined to rob it of nationalist support.

Bloody Sunday

The government's response to the growing violence was to introduce internment (imprisonment without trial) of **terrorist** suspects. Almost all of those arrested were Catholics, even though Protestant gunmen were also operating in the province. (The **paramilitary Ulster Defence Association** or UDA was set up in September 1971 in response to the activities of the **Provos**.) The arrests stirred up bitter resentment among even moderate **nationalists**.

Catholic confidence in the British army's impartiality reached a new low on 30 January 1972, a day that became known as 'Bloody Sunday'. That afternoon, British **paratroopers** shot dead thirteen unarmed civilians – a fourteenth died of his wounds later – during minor street disturbances following a peaceful **civil rights** march through the streets of Londonderry. Although the army consistently claimed that its men came under fire first, no arms were found and no soldiers were wounded.

Moderate Catholic opinion was outraged by the events of Bloody Sunday. But when a **UK** government enquiry effectively cleared the paratroopers of any blame or wrongdoing, the community exploded with fury. Support for the Provos soared, and the voices of moderate Catholics seeking democratic ways of living harmoniously with their Protestant neighbours were largely drowned out. The two communities now seemed hopelessly divided.

Young members of the Ulster Defence Association (UDA) use an illegal radio station to transmit an anti-nationalist message from a home in Belfast's Shankhill Road, a heartland of the **loyalist** movement.

Under fire

One English observer of the events of Bloody Sunday was Simon Winchester, a journalist with the *Guardian* newspaper. Here he reports on what he saw when British paratroopers interrupted a protest meeting that began as the march ended.

Mourners carry crosses commemorating some of the fourteen civilians killed by British troops on Bloody Sunday.

Four or five armoured cars appeared at William Street, and raced into the Rossville Street square, and several thousand people began to run away . . . Paratroopers piled out of their vehicles, many ran forward to make arrests, but others rushed to the street corners. It was these men, perhaps twenty in all, who opened the fire with their rifles. I saw three men fall to the ground. One was still obviously alive with blood pumping from his leg. The others, both apparently in their teens, seemed dead.

The meeting at Free Derry Corner broke up in hysteria as thousands of people either ran or dived for the ground.

Army snipers could be seen firing continuously towards the central Bogside streets and at one stage a lone army sniper fired two shots at me as I peered around a corner. One shot chipped a large chunk of masonry from a wall behind me.

Then people could be seen moving forward in Fahan Street, their hands above their heads. One man was carrying a white handkerchief. Gunfire was directed even at them and they fled or fell to the ground.

Direct rule

Bloody Sunday was a disaster not only for the individuals concerned but also for **UK** policy in Northern Ireland. The army had been sent to the province as a neutral force to keep the warring sides apart. But it met with extreme provocation from the **Provos** – almost fifty soldiers had died as a result of **terrorist** action during the previous year. Under the onslaught, it shed its apparent neutrality and came to be seen, by the Catholic community at least, as firmly inclined to the **loyalist** side. Clearly the Provos had won the propaganda battle for many Catholic hearts and minds.

The immediate result of the shootings was an upsurge in violence. In all, 467 people would die in 1972, easily the highest total for any year of the Troubles. Abroad, there was an increase in support for the Catholic cause. In the Republic of Ireland, the British Embassy was burned down, while in the USA, fundraisers collecting money from Irish-Americans to support **nationalist** groups, including the **IRA**, found that contributions more than doubled.

The political effects in Northern Ireland were even more dramatic. On 24 March 1972, less than two months after the Bloody Sunday shootings, the UK Prime Minister Edward Heath announced that the Stormont parliament was to be suspended and that the UK government would take over responsibility for running the province. After more than fifty years of partial self-government, Northern Ireland was once more to be ruled directly from **Westminster**.

A political solution. . .

On 24 March 1972, Prime Minister Edward Heath announces to the House of Commons that he is imposing direct rule on Northern Ireland from London.

We were concerned about the present provision of responsibility for law and order between Belfast and Westminster whereby control remains largely with the Northern Ireland government while operational responsibility rests mainly with the British army, and therefore with the United Kingdom government. This responsibility is not merely domestic; it is a matter of international concern as well. . . The United Kingdom government remained of the view that the transfer of this responsibility to Westminster was an indispensable condition for progress in finding a political solution to Northern Ireland.

The Northern Ireland government's position therefore leaves [the UK government] with no alternative to assuming full and direct responsibility for the administration of Northern Ireland until a political solution to the problems of the province can be worked out in consultation with all those concerned. Parliament will therefore be invited to pass before Easter a measure transferring all legislative and executive powers now vested in the Northern Ireland parliament and government to the United Kingdom Parliament and a United Kingdom minister.

Police examine the results of an IRA bomb explosion in central London in 1973 that killed one man and wounded 238 people. From 1972 on, bombs planted in mainland Britain claimed many civilian lives.

Power sharing fails

By imposing direct rule, Edward Heath hoped to redeem military failure by a bold political move. The plan was to introduce a new governmental structure for the province in which Protestants and Catholics would share power. In December 1973, a four-day conference held at Sunningdale in Berkshire, England, hammered out the terms of the deal. It was attended by representatives of the Irish government and by moderate Northern Ireland politicians.

Leading Northern Ireland politicians including the **Ulster Unionist** Prime Minister Brian Faulkner attend a session of the Sunningdale Conference in 1973. The conference approved plans for a power sharing executive that came to nothing as a result of a loyalist workers' strike.

The **power sharing** arrangement represented the best chance for peace in the province in a generation, but it was bitterly opposed by **militant loyalists**. They saw it as just the sort of surrender to Catholic demands that Ian Paisley and his supporters had always refused to contemplate. In response, they called a general strike that effectively brought the province to a halt.

The leaders of the power sharing executive pleaded in vain with the **UK** Prime Minister (now Labour's Harold Wilson again) to send in troops to break the strike. After two weeks of growing disruption, they gave up the struggle. Their chief, Brian Faulkner, resigned, along with his moderate **unionist** colleagues. The power sharing experiment had collapsed before it had even had a chance to get started.

'Sunningdale sellout'

Following the collapse of the power sharing executive, the Ulster Workers' Council (UWC) – the body that had organized the general strike – published a newsletter justifying its actions. It explained the strikers' motives and what they thought they had gained.

The constitutional stoppage in May 1974 was a concerted victory for the **Ulster** loyalist people, after years of **republican** rebellion - and political deceit by the then leaders of the Official Unionist Party and the **Westminster** government. In the wake of the constitutional stoppage, Westminster belatedly realized that the ordinary people of Ulster could not and would not accept the Sunningdale sellout.

In particular, the Labour government were suddenly aware of the power of the Ulster workers which had been mobilized by the UWC and they plainly got the message that . . . some of the full-time officials of British-based **trade unions** were completely out of step with the ordinary workers. It is a bold fact that many of these full-time officials were using their position within the trade union movement to further political aspirations which were totally alien to the trade union membership at large.

What did we gain from the stoppage?

Firstly, we regained our dignity as loyalists after years of treason, double-dealing and appeasement.

Secondly, we reminded [British Prime Minister] Harold Wilson and his colleagues in government, that Ulster workers (just like their fellow-workers in Britain) could not be pushed around like sheep.

Thirdly, we reminded Britain that Ulster's loyalty could not be taken for granted - it must be earned!

Finally, we killed Sunningdale with its many trappings and got a pledge from Westminster on fresh elections to an Ulster Constitutional Convention.

The dirty war

With the collapse of **power sharing**, any prospect of a political
solution to the Troubles was effectively postponed for a decade. The
crisis had produced a bloody stalemate with no apparent way out. As
paramilitaries on both sides continued to commit atrocities, the
security forces tried to contain the violence by working with
informers who could give them advance warning of planned **terrorist**
actions. This shadowy undercover war would eventually lead to
accusations that some people in the forces had direct dealings with
terrorists. In particular, **republicans** accused the **UK** security service
of working with paramilitary groups.

Bombings and shootings continued not only in Northern Ireland but
also in the Irish Republic and mainland Britain, where the **IRA** sought
to spread terror in order to influence public opinion to get the troops
withdrawn. Horrified by the violence, some people found expression
in the Peace Movement, which for a time brought Protestant and
Catholic moderates in the province together. The two Catholic women,
Mairead Corrigan and Betty Williams, who founded the Peace Movement
received the Nobel Peace Prize in 1976, but sadly the killings continued.

Although most Northern Ireland Catholics supported the **Provisional
IRA**'s goal of a united Ireland, only a small minority agreed that
violence should be used to achieve it. One development that did win
wider sympathy for the Provos, however, was a series of hunger
strikes in 1981. Ten men, imprisoned for belonging to the IRA, starved
themselves to death in protest at the government's refusal to treat
them as political prisoners. After their deaths, there was a marked
increase in electoral
support for **Sinn Fein**,
the IRA's political wing.

Peace activists Betty Williams (left) and
Mairead Corrigan (right) lead a march in
Belfast in 1976. The two women shared
the Nobel Peace Prize that year for
their campaign against violence.

Hunger strike

Laurence McKeown, one of the IRA hunger strikers who survived the 1981 campaign, describes a meeting with his family sixty days into his fast. The strikers were protesting at the UK government's refusal to grant them special status as political prisoners. Such status would have given them improved conditions, including the right to wear their own clothes, to meet with other prisoners, and to avoid prison work duties.

My mother came in, sister, brother, my father and different uncles. And I think all of them, except my mother, asked me to come off the hunger strike. I was still lucid at that time. There was a lot of crying and a lot of silences.

I can remember the morning of the sixty-ninth day, when I got some time with my mother. I was probably just dozing off, sleeping and waking up, and when I was waking up I was lucid. My mother had been a bit religious, not in a big way but she had a sort of quiet faith, I suppose you would say. I remember her saying to me, 'You know what you've to do and I do what I've to do.' That was the way it was left between us. I think what my mother meant was that it was God's will and if it ended up in a situation where I was in a coma, then she would act to save my life. I didn't pursue it any further, as I thought I would just die instantly.

Apparently, on the evening of the sixty-ninth day I was talking to people who weren't there, and calling people by the wrong names. On the morning of the seventieth day the doctors were looking for certain reflexes and I wasn't responding in any way. And I think about noon, my mother authorized medical intervention. There had already been several people this had happened to: I was the last one that it happened to because the hunger strike ended a few weeks afterwards. I had a whole mixture of emotions. I can't say I was happy to be alive, but I certainly couldn't say I was sad to be alive. I was alive, I wasn't even thinking about what was going to happen in the future.

The Hillsborough Accord

When political progress was at last made, it came from an unexpected source. Margaret Thatcher, Conservative Prime Minister of the **UK**, was a particular target of **republican** anger because of her unyielding treatment of the **IRA** hunger strikers. She had been the intended victim of a bombing which killed four people at the Conservative Party annual conference in Brighton, England in 1984. Although she had no sympathy with Irish **nationalism**, Thatcher was wise enough to heed warnings from Garret Fitzgerald, Taoseiach (Prime Minister) of the Irish **Republic**. Fitzgerald told her of the dangers posed by the rise in electoral support for **Sinn Fein** among Northern Ireland's Catholics. This support, he said, implied a growing sympathy for the **Provos** and for terrorism.

In 1985, as a result of these concerns, the UK and Irish governments signed the Anglo-Irish Agreement at Hillsborough Castle near Belfast. This document (also known as the Hillsborough Accord) reasserted that there should be no change in Northern Ireland's constitutional status without the consent of the Protestant majority. However, it also gave the Irish Republic a voice in the province's affairs, to guarantee that the rights of the Catholic minority would be upheld.

The Hillsborough Accord caused outrage among **loyalists** who wanted nothing to do with a wider Ireland. They made an immediate attempt to overturn it, taking strike action in the hope that this would lead to victory as it had in 1975. This time, however, Northern Ireland's police force faced down the strikers. Even so, **unionist** anger was sufficiently strong to bring down a new Northern Ireland assembly, which had tentatively been set up to provide a political voice for the province. Once more, **power sharing** seemed to have failed.

Garret Fitzgerald and Margaret Thatcher, the prime ministers of Ireland and Britain, exchange documents after signing the Anglo-Irish Agreement at Hillsborough Castle, south of Belfast, in 1985.

The horror of terrorism

Protestant anger at what loyalists saw as the Hillsborough sellout was fuelled by outrage at continuing IRA atrocities against civilians. Here Unionist MP William McCrea writes to the Hollywood actor Micky Rourke, a known supporter of the IRA. McCrea describes the murders of his cousins Rachel and Robert McLernon, aged sixteen and twenty-one, who were killed in a bomb attack in 1976.

A car had gone over a hedge, and Rachel and her friends went to help whoever was inside. But there was nobody, and somebody immediately shouted: 'Watch, maybe there's a bomb.' They climbed back on to the road, and Rachel and Robert pointed to something in the field. At that moment an IRA bomb exploded and Rachel and Robert were blown to bits. I remember the face of Rachel in the mortuary when I went to identify her. She had become engaged to be married that day and she was a beauty queen. I looked down upon her and saw half of her face blown off. Her brother lay to the right-hand side. He was in a small plastic bag stacked against a table. He didn't even get on to the table, because there wasn't sufficient of him left. As I looked upon them I can assure you there was nothing glorious and nothing beautiful about the handiwork of **terrorism**... Two years later their mother Shirley died of a broken heart at the age of forty-three. I was with her right up until the minute she died. She kept saying to me: 'William, two of my children left me one night and I have waited for them to return every day since then.' She saw the two coffins. They were sealed. They had to be. I was the only one who saw them and so she didn't accept their deaths. Her death, Mr Rourke, is not to be found in the statistics listing the victims of violence.

Republican sympathizers attending the funeral of three IRA activists shot by British troops take cover as a lone loyalist gunman attacks the mourners with grenades and gunfire. Three people were killed in this 1988 assault.

Seeds of hope

Although the attempt at **power sharing** had failed, seeds of hope were starting to germinate in the late 1980s and early 1990s. One important development was that, despite continuing its campaign of bombings, the **IRA** was also fostering a new interest in electoral politics through its political arm, **Sinn Fein**. Another was a growing war-weariness that helped to persuade all but die-hard extremists on both sides that violence offered no long-term solution to the problems in Northern Ireland.

In 1991, talks involving all the major parties apart from Sinn Fein began at Stormont. Although the public debate achieved little, some old enemies were in fact talking to each other elsewhere in private.

A major shift
Denis Bradley, a former Catholic priest, served as a go-between in secret negotiations involving the IRA and the UK government in the early 1990s. Here he describes to a television interviewer events in November 1990 that signalled the beginning of a breakthrough in attitudes. 'Fred' is the false name of Bradley's UK government contact.

The leader of the **Social Democratic and Labour Party (SDLP)**, John Hume – a Catholic and a **nationalist**, but committed to achieving change by democratic means – held discussions with Gerry Adams, leader of Sinn Fein and a suspected IRA man. More controversially, the **UK** government was also establishing secret contacts with Sinn Fein leaders, to try to find a way of ending the violence. From 1992, the peace process was further encouraged by US President Bill Clinton, who played an active part in bringing the different factions together.

Surrounded by television cameramen, Gerry Adams, the chief spokesman for the IRA's political wing, Sinn Fein, arrives for talks at the Northern Ireland parliament building at Stormont in 1999. The discussions aimed to establish a framework for a new power sharing executive.

Children play in front of a mural advertising the Ulster Freedom Fighters (UFF). This Protestant **paramilitary** group was declared illegal in 1973.

Fred came with a speech which [Britain's Northern Ireland minister] Peter Brooke was about to deliver, and said this was an indicator of goodwill, of their willingness to re-engage and to begin the process of building up some semblance – small as it may be – of trust between republicanism and the British government. He said this speech was going to be delivered in a couple of days' time. Would we please get it to the **republican** movement, so that they can have it to know that it's happening, because we believe that the content is extremely important.

I read the content, and there was a statement within it that the British had no selfish or strategic position within Northern Ireland, that they wanted to be reasonably neutral and that they wanted to try to work out a solution. Now that's only a sentence, but within this type of reality that type of sentence has major implications. Because if you analyze this historically, it is the first time ever that the British government said, 'We have no selfish and strategic position vis-à-vis Northern Ireland, we are people who want peace, we want to work out a solution within Northern Ireland.'

And I thought there was a basis for a solution, it was there within that document. Peter Brooke was not alone giving this document, but he was actually beginning to use what I would call tonality – the way he said things was very different from what was being said in the late 1980s.

Republicans took it, and I remember talking to [IRA leader Martin] McGuinness afterwards, who read the sentence and interpreted the sentence extremely well. He said: 'Yes, if that is true that is a major, major shift.' Now he didn't trust it, had major reservations about it, it's only words on paper, what does it mean? But you could see that things were changing, and that things could begin to happen.

The Good Friday Agreement

The various peace initiatives under way in the early 1990s bore fruit in 1998, with the signing of the Good Friday Agreement. Unlike its predecessors, this accord was signed by representatives of **Sinn Fein** as well as by members of the parties on both sides traditionally committed to democratic policies.

What had changed was that the **IRA** had, in 1994, given a commitment to cease all military activities. And, although the truce broke down in 1996–97, it was subsequently restored. **Loyalist paramilitaries**, who by the early 1990s were killing more people than the IRA, responded by announcing a ceasefire of their own. Even so, agreement was only reached following strong pressure on politicians of all persuasions from the new **UK** Prime Minister Tony Blair and from US President Bill Clinton, who took a deep personal interest in resolving the conflict.

Under the terms of the agreement, a National Assembly was set up to provide a **power sharing** executive for the province. Various cross-border organizations were set up to increase co-operation between Northern Ireland and the Irish **Republic** in fields such as tourism and agriculture. A commission was appointed to study ways of making Northern Ireland's policing more acceptable to the Catholic community, and the UK agreed to speed up the release of paramilitary prisoners. Apart from the crucial inclusion of Sinn Fein, the 1998 settlement was not radically different from those that had been rejected in 1975 and 1985. Sadly, it had been necessary for 23 years of bloodshed to elapse to get the political process back where it had begun.

Demonstrators make their point in 1996 outside the Northern Ireland parliament building at Stormont, where talks were being held to decide the future of the province. The Good Friday Agreement two years later was a result of these discussions.

Nothing to fear. . .

One week after coming to power in 1997, UK Prime Minister Tony Blair visited Belfast to try to reassure Northern Ireland's Protestant community that power sharing with Catholics and co-operation with the Republic of Ireland did not mean a betrayal of their interests. In his speech he emphasized repeatedly that there would be no change in the province's status against the wishes of a majority of the population.

Northern Ireland is a part of the United Kingdom because that is the wish of a majority of the people who live here. It will remain part of the United Kingdom for as long as that remains the case. This principle of consent is and will be at the heart of my Government's policies on Northern Ireland. It is the key principle.

It means that there can be absolutely no possibility of a change in the status of Northern Ireland as a part of the United Kingdom without the clear and formal consent of a majority of the people of Northern Ireland. Any settlement must be negotiated [by the Northern Ireland political parties], not imposed; it must be endorsed by the people of Northern Ireland in a **referendum**; and it must be endorsed by the British Parliament.

Of course, those who wish to see a united Ireland without coercion can argue for it, not least in the talks. If they succeeded, we would certainly respect that. But none of us in this hall today, even the youngest, is likely to see Northern Ireland as anything but a part of the United Kingdom. That is the reality, because the consent principle is now almost universally accepted. . . So fears of betrayal are simply misplaced. **Unionists** have nothing to fear from a new Labour government. A political settlement is not a slippery slope to a united Ireland. The government will not be persuaders for unity.

A fragile peace

The Good Friday Agreement was put to the vote in both the Irish **Republic** and in Northern Ireland. In the Irish Republic, 94.4 per cent of voters supported it, but in Northern Ireland only 71.1 per cent did. This was because, while about 95 per cent of Northern Ireland's Catholics voted in favour, only 55 per cent of Protestants did. A National Assembly was summoned, but the **power sharing** executive proved hard to implement as the various groups could not agree on its membership.

In the years that followed, the Agreement mostly succeeded in stopping the killings in Northern Ireland. Relations between the Catholic and Protestant communities improved markedly, although the summer marching season continued to provide an annual flashpoint. Now, though, when **loyalist** marchers sought to parade through Catholic areas they often found their way blocked by the security forces.

At the beginning of the new century, the peace in Northern Ireland remained fragile. In particular, the issue of the decommissioning (declaration and destruction) of **terrorist** weapons continued to loom large. The Protestant community generally believed it had made the greatest concessions for peace, and insisted that the **IRA** had to be seen to have disarmed if there was to be a lasting end to violence. The IRA's slowness to comply led to **unionist** threats to halt the entire peace process. For all the progress made, Northern Ireland remained a deeply divided community. Only the fear of returning to what had gone before kept the two sides talking.

Demonstrators hold up paper doves symbolizing peace at a 1996 Belfast rally. The protest was called in response to an IRA bombing in the Docklands area of London two days earlier that had killed two people.

A vision for the future

In 1999 the **UK** and Irish governments asked US President Bill Clinton's peace envoy George Mitchell, a former US Senator, to review progress on the peace agreement. Mitchell insisted on bringing representatives of the two sides face to face. Here two lifelong enemies – the unionist MP Ken Maginnis and the IRA leader Martin McGuinness – describe a small incident that showed how attitudes could change.

Ken Maginnis:
George Mitchell would work with intensive discussions until dinner time, and then he would have us in to dinner, so really for the first time some of us were sitting down, 'socially', with **Sinn Fein**-IRA. It was a strange experience. Once George looked at Martin McGuinness, and then he looked at me and he'd say, 'You two must be related - Maginnis, McGuinness - there must be a relationship?' And I remember saying to him, 'I know mine's the Celtic name - Martin's is the Anglo-Irish.'

Martin McGuinness laughed, and maybe for the first time I saw him ever really laugh. Let me put it like this, it probably didn't change Martin McGuinness's attitude to me: he sees me as part of the **establishment**. It doesn't change my attitude to him: I see him as the active IRA man. What it probably does is demonstrate that if we hadn't been such poles apart, we might actually have been able to laugh together, to talk together. It didn't make a personal change for us, but I think it could perhaps have given us a vision for the future. Our children, or our children's children, perhaps won't have this animosity and distrust.

Martin McGuinness:
Ken trying to claim that he was more Irish than I was - I thought it was grand, it was great. Eventually, as the conversations moved on, Ken brought in photographs of his grandchildren and showed them to me, and talked to me about his family and about his son. That was probably the first real sensible conversation that I had had with Ken Maginnis, even though I'd heard about him and known about him for many years. So that was progress.

What have we learnt from the Troubles?

There were no winners in the Troubles, only losers. The **IRA** failed in its attempt to force the British to withdraw from Ireland. The **unionists** were eventually forced to make concessions to the Catholic community. Such concessions had long been bitterly resisted by the **loyalists**. The Catholics gained the principle of equal treatment with the Protestants, but failed to secure the union with southern Ireland that the majority of the Irish population had always wanted.

Just as significantly for the long term, Northern Ireland as a whole stagnated. Its economy lagged behind that of the rest of the **UK**. In 1997, average earnings in the province were almost 15 per cent lower than those in England. The contrast with southern Ireland was even more marked. Buoyed by European Union membership, the **Republic**'s economy soared, transforming what had been an economically backward agricultural land into the continent's fastest-growing nation.

In fact, Northern Ireland stood still while the world around it was changing. Yet if the Troubles have proved anything, it is that the province cannot stand apart from the rest of the world. Increasingly it is bound in to a wider community, by television and the Internet and by the ease of international travel. The best hope for the future is that the members of a new generation, aware of the wider opportunities available to them, will look forward with hope rather than back to the past with all its murderous hatreds.

An unemployed man watches youths playing street soccer in Londonderry in 1955. At the time, the unemployment rate in the city had reached 20 percent.

A new beginning

US President Bill Clinton played a significant role in encouraging the peace process in Northern Ireland. These excerpts are from a speech he made in Belfast in September 1998, addressing members of the Northern Ireland Assembly, which was set up following the Good Friday Agreement.

For 30 long years the Troubles took a terrible toll: too many died, too many families grieved, every family was denied the quiet blessings of a normal life and the constant fear that a simple trip to the store could be devastated by bombs and bullets... From here on the destiny of Northern Ireland is in the hands of its people and its representatives [in the Northern Ireland Assembly]. From farming to finance, education to healthcare, this new assembly has the opportunity and the obligation to forge the future.

Belfast's Lagan Weir is illuminated at night. The flood defence barrier, which forms part of a major docklands development project, symbolizes the new prosperity that the 1990s brought to the city and to Northern Ireland as a whole.

So much more unites you than divides you – the values of faith and family, work and community, the same land and heritage, the same love of laughter and language. You aspire to the same things – to live in peace and security, to provide for your loved ones, to build a better life and pass on brighter possibilities to your children. These are not Catholic or Protestant dreams, these are human dreams, to be realized best together.

51

Timeline

1171	England's King Henry II claims overlordship in Ireland.
1534	England's King Henry VIII breaks with the Pope in Rome.
1611	The **plantation** of Ulster.
1690	William of Orange defeats the Catholic James II at the Battle of the Boyne.
1801	The **Act of Union** makes Ireland an integral part of the **United Kingdom**, along with England, Wales and Scotland.
1845–48	The Great Famine kills one million Irish men, women and children.
1920	The Government of Ireland Act creates separate parliaments for Northern and southern Ireland.
1921	After two years of war, the **Irish Free State** is established in southern Ireland.
1949	Southern Ireland breaks its last remaining links with the UK to become the fully independent **Republic** of Ireland.
1965	Reforming Northern Irish Prime Minister Terence O'Neill agrees to meet the Taoiseach (Prime Minister) of the Irish Republic – the first such meeting since the foundation of Northern Ireland.
1967	Foundation of the Northern Ireland Civil Rights Association to campaign for an end to discrimination against Catholics.
1969	January: **loyalists** attack a **civil rights** march near Londonderry.
	August: rioting in Londonderry (the 'Battle of the Bogside') and in Belfast results in British troops being sent to Northern Ireland.
1970	The **Provisional IRA** splits from the official **IRA** to pursue a more **militant** armed campaign against the British forces.
1971	The UK government introduces internment of **terrorist** suspects.
1972	30 January: fourteen unarmed demonstrators are shot dead in Londonderry by British troops on 'Bloody Sunday'.
	March: in face of a rising tide of violence, the UK government imposes direct rule from **Westminster** on Northern Ireland.
1973	**Power sharing** proposed between Protestants and Catholics at Sunningdale.
1974	**Ulster** Workers' Council strike brings about the collapse of the power sharing executive. Westminster resumes direct rule.
1976	Peace Movement founded to protest against the continuing violence.
1981	IRA prisoners die on hunger strike while demanding political prisoner status.
1982	**Sinn Fein** wins 10 per cent of the vote in elections to a new Northern Ireland National Assembly.
1984	An IRA bomb kills four people at the Conservative Party conference in Brighton.
1985	The Anglo-Irish Agreement (also known as the Hillsborough Accord) is signed.
1991	Talks start between all Northern Ireland's major political parties except Sinn Fein.
1994	The IRA announces a ceasefire.
1995	US President Bill Clinton visits Belfast.
1998	April: the Good Friday Agreement commits Northern Ireland to power sharing and cross-border co-operation with the Republic of Ireland.
	August: dissident **republicans** calling themselves the Real IRA explode a bomb that kills 28 shoppers and tourists in Omagh, Northern Ireland.
1999	Power sharing executive established. Westminster again devolves power to Northern Ireland Assembly.
2000	Power sharing executive is suspended following **unionist** protests about the IRA's reluctance to give details of weapons it has decommissioned.
2003	Fresh attempts to restore power sharing continue to founder on the issue of weapons decommissioning.

Find out more

Books & websites

Lives in Crisis: Conflict in Northern Ireland, R. G. Grant, (Hodder, 2001).
Turning Points in History: The Irish Famine, Tony Allan, (Heinemann Library, 2001).
Troubled World: The Troubles in Northern Ireland, Ivan Minnis, (Heinemann Library, 2001).

http://www.bbc.co.uk/history/war/troubles
A BBC site with a timeline, a gallery of mural paintings, and audio clips of songs and interviews.

http://www.cain.ulst.ac.uk
By far the most detailed site on all aspects of the Troubles. Aimed at adults, but full of useful information.

List of primary sources

The author and publisher gratefully acknowledge the following publications and websites from which written sources in the book are drawn. In some cases the wording or sentence structure has been simplified to make the material more appropriate for a school readership.

P. 9 From the Brigham Young University website.
P. 11 From the UK Public Record Office website.
P. 13 From the CAIN website.
P. 15 Quoted in *The Great Hunger* by Cecil Woodham-Smith, Penguin Books, London, 1991, page 162.
P. 17 From An Unknown Country by Mrs Craik, 1880. Quoted in *The Oxford Book of Ireland*, edited by Patricia Craig, Oxford University Press, London and New York, 1998, page 223.
P. 19 From the CAIN website.
P. 21 The words of Padraig Pearse, quoted in *The Easter Rebellion* by Max Caulfield, Frederick Muller Ltd, London, 1964, pages 98-99.
P. 23 From *Come Day, Go Day, God Send Sunday: The songs and life story of a traditional singer and farmer from Co. Fermanagh*, collated by Robin Morton, 1973. Quoted here from *The Oxford Book of Ireland*, edited by Patricia Craig, Oxford University Press, Oxford & New York, 1998, page 302.
P. 25 The words of Conn McLuskey quoted in *The Troubles* by Tim Pat Coogan, Arrow Books, London, 1996.
P. 27 *Burntollet* by Bowes Egan and Vincent McCormack, LRS Publishers, 1969.
P. 29 The words of Edna Hanson quoted in *May the Lord in His Mercy Be Kind to Belfast* by Tony Parker, Jonathan Cape, London, 1993, pages 295-6.
P. 31 *Brits Speak Out: British Soldiers' Impressions of the Northern Ireland Conflict* compiled by John Lindsay, Guildhall Press, 1998.
P. 33 *Poems 1956–86* by James Simmons, The Gallery Press, 1986.
P. 35 The words of Simon Winchester quoted in *The Troubles* by Tim Pat Coogan, Arrow Books, London, 1996, page 161.
P. 37 From the CAIN website.

P. 39 From Issue 1 of the *UWC Journal – the Voice of the Ulster Workers' Council*, as reproduced on the CAIN website.

P. 41 *Endgame in Ireland* by Eamonn Mallie and David McKittrick, Hodder & Stoughton, 2001.

P. 43 *The Irish War* by Tony Geraghty, HarperCollins, London, 1998.

P. 45 *Endgame in Ireland* by Eamonn Mallie and David McKittrick, Hodder & Stoughton, 2001.

P. 47 *The Northern Ireland Peace Process* by Thomas Hennessey, Gill & Macmillan, Dublin, 2000.

P. 49 *Endgame in Ireland* by Eamonn Mallie and David McKittrick, Hodder & Stoughton, 2001.

P. 51 President Bill Clinton's Keynote Address at the Waterfront Hotel, Belfast, 3 September 1998. Quoted here from the CAIN website.

Glossary

Act of Union   British law that in 1801 joined Ireland to England, Scotland and Wales as part of the United Kingdom

alleviate   to lighten or improve

Apprentice Boys of Derry   loyalist group that marches each year to commemorate the Siege of Londonderry in 1688, when the city's apprentices closed the town gates against the army of the Catholic King James II

assassination   murder for political ends

auxiliary   member of an additional troop called up to reinforce a regular army

B Specials   part-time armed police force set up to combat the IRA. Always regarded as anti-Catholic, the force was abolished in 1969.

civil rights   rights to equal treatment with other citizens under the law

Crown   the British monarch, also officially the head of state of all Ireland until 1949, when the Republic of Ireland was established

curfew   order preventing people from leaving their homes at certain hours (usually overnight)

Dark Ages   the period between the collapse of the Roman Empire and the Middle Ages, from about AD 400 to 1000, traditionally seen as a time of ignorance and backwardness

emancipation   granting people full civil rights

emigrate   to start a new life abroad

establishment, the   ruling powers-that-be

eviction   expulsion by landlords of tenants from their lands and homes

Fenian Brotherhood   underground nationalist organization, set up in the mid-19th century, and prepared to use violence to win independence for Ireland

Gaelic   language of the Celtic people in Ireland

government bill   proposal, brought forward by the government in Parliament, to change the law

home rule   self-government for Ireland, as sought by Irish nationalists from the mid-19th century to 1920

Irish Free State   name given to the Republic of Ireland between 1921 and 1937, when it had won the right to self-government but remained a part of the British Empire

Irish Republican Army (IRA)   nationalist armed force that fought for Irish independence in 1919–21 and that continued to fight for a united Ireland thereafter, even though declared illegal in both Northern Ireland and the Irish Republic

loyalist   Northern Ireland Protestant who swears loyalty to the UK

martyr   someone who gives his or her life for a political or religious cause

militant   aggressive support for, or supporter of, a cause

nationalist   in Northern Ireland, an individual (usually Catholic) whose loyalties lie with the Republic of Ireland rather than with the UK

Orange Order   society originally set up in 1795 to celebrate the victory of the Protestant King William of Orange over the Catholic King James II in 1690. Its supporters, known as Orangemen, hold marches and parades each summer.

paramilitary   member of an illegal armed organization such as the Catholic IRA or the Protestant UDA

paratrooper member of a parachute regiment (one whose soldiers are trained for airborne attack)

Penal Laws series of laws passed by the British in the 18th century that severely disadvantaged Irish Catholics

plantation the settling of immigrant communities in selected areas of a country for political purposes

power sharing the sharing of power between Protestant and Catholic communities, usually by guaranteeing each one an agreed number of representatives in the ruling executive (group)

Protestant ascendancy period in the 18th century when the Penal Laws deprived Catholics of most civil rights and Protestant rule in Ireland went almost unchallenged

Provisional IRA (Provos) militant wing of the IRA that broke away from the official IRA in 1969 and became the main republican terrorist force

Puritans in the 17th century, extreme Protestants passionately opposed to the Catholic Church

radical describes a huge change or a supporter of such change

referendum vote in which electors are asked to agree or disagree on a specific question

Reformation split in the Church in the 16th century that divided Christians into Protestants and Catholics

repeal undo existing laws

republic country ruled by a president or other elected official, not by a king or queen

republican in Northern Ireland, an individual – usually, but not exclusively, Catholic – seeking to break the province's links with the British Crown

reunification in Ireland, the reuniting of Northern Ireland and the Republic of Ireland into a single country

Royal Ulster Constabulary (RUC) Northern Ireland's police force

Sinn Fein Irish republican party now regarded as the political wing of the Provisional IRA

Social Democratic and Labour Party (SDLP) main moderate Catholic political party in Northern Ireland, committed to achieving a united Ireland by peaceful means

terrorist someone who seeks to achieve political ends by spreading terror among the civilian population

trade union organization of workers joined to protect their political or economic interests

Twelfth of July day on which the Orange Order has traditionally celebrated William of Orange's victory at the Battle of the Boyne in 1690, starting the annual 'marching season' of loyalist parades and processions

Ulster historically, one of the four main provinces of Ireland. Now often used to mean Northern Ireland, which was formed from six of the nine counties of Ulster in 1921.

Ulster Defence Association (UDA) largest Protestant paramilitary group for much of the Troubles, formed in 1971 and only declared illegal in 1992

Ulster Defence Regiment (UDR) locally recruited militia, set up in 1970 to replace the B Specials and placed under the control of the British army

Ulster Unionist Party Northern Ireland's largest political party, dedicated to retaining the province's links with Britain inside the United Kingdom

Ulster Volunteer Force (UVF) originally set up in 1912 to oppose Irish independence, the UVF was revived as a Protestant terrorist organization in 1966 and was subsequently declared illegal

unionist supporter of continuing links with the United Kingdom

Union Jack national flag of the United Kingdom, an important emblem for loyalists

United Kingdom (UK) the island of Britain – made up of England, Scotland and Wales – together with Northern Ireland. It became the United Kingdom of Great Britain and Northern Ireland in 1921, after the rest of Ireland was declared the Irish Free State.

usurpation illegal seizure of power

Westminster seat of the United Kingdom's Parliament in London

Index